Getting Into Physical Therapy School:

10 Essential Things You Must Do

Nicholas Gallo, PT, DPT

Disclaimer

The contents of this book are based on my personal experiences applying to Physical Therapy School and are for informational purposes only. Admission into a Physical Therapy program cannot be guaranteed by reading this book. This book does not constitute medical advice; the content of this book is not intended to be a substitute for professional medical advice, diagnosis, or treatment. Always seek the advice of a physician or other qualified health provider with any questions you may have regarding a medical condition. Never disregard professional medical advice or delay in seeking it because of something you have read on this website. Reliance on any information provided by this book is solely at your own risk.

Getting Into Physical Therapy School:
10 Essential Things You Must Do

In today's academic society, it is extremely important to try and strengthen your application as much as possible in order to separate yourself from others. I don't want to scare you, but when I applied to PT school, I know my alma mater received hundreds of applications and they selected only 40 students. I personally know some people who would have been great colleagues in the PT world but who were not selected during this admission process. It's a shame, but the truth is, there are hundreds of great candidates out there all going after the same spot. I also know people, however, who applied and were accepted into Physical Therapy school by utilizing these strategies. Their applications were stronger, and they were able to separate themselves from the competition. I will never forget the stresses and times of self-doubt when applying to physical therapy school. There were so many steps and rules to follow that at times I truly felt lost.

I have written this guide to provide prospective Physical Therapy students out there with the knowledge and framework necessary for applying to Physical Therapy school. Back when I was an undergraduate student, I did not have any knowledge on how to try and apply to school or bolster my application. I went with the arrogant mentality, "Oh I'll get in," which is a HUGE mistake. You might be an excellent candidate, but there may be certain areas of your application that need improvement. Because of my cockiness and arrogance, I was waitlisted the first time I applied; however, I was not accepted. I assumed I had a very strong application when, in fact, there were several areas I needed to work on. Between the time I was rejected and the second time I applied, I implemented many strategies to strengthen my application and provide a lot of evidence for myself as to why I would be a great candidate. I was put on my target school's waitlist the second time around, but this time I was accepted! Therefore, in this publication, I want to show you how to look for areas to improve on, how to fix them, and how to separate yourself from the competition. At the end of each section, I will summarize the mistakes I made the first time I applied and the improvements I made my second time applying so that you may use them to your advantage in your application strategy.

Finally, I would like to point out that I offer free educational videos showing a variety of different treatments and diagnoses on my YouTube channel Physical Therapy 101. This channel was started to provide free, to-the-point exercises to patients and practitioners. It can also be a great benefit to prospective students. This channel is continuously being updated and provides a slew of information spanning several diagnoses, so please subscribe if you are interested. Supplemental information can be found on our website www.physicaltherapy101.net.

Table of Contents

———

1

Using PTCAS Effectively

To start the entire application you must go to the Physical Therapist Centralized Application Service, also known as PTCAS. This is your greatest asset in the entire process, but it can also be your greatest adversary if not used properly and effectively. It can be found at www.ptcas.org. It is important to note that not all schools participate in PTCAS, so if the school you are interested in does not, you most likely need to visit that university's website to get the details. However, in my experience, all the schools I was interested in were listed on PTCAS and I am fairly certain that the majority are at this point.

Step 1: Find the school you are interested in attending

This probably goes without saying, but it's important to find the school(s) you are interested in. PTCAS includes schools from all over the United States, and if that school uses PTCAS, you will be able to find it. PTCAS is very organized in that it lists schools by state and by name. Once you locate your school, PTCAS provides a copious amount of information related to that PT program. It is imperative that you know every piece of information!

Finding more than one target school is important because the more places you apply to, the more chances you have at getting accepted.

Step 2: Look at that program's details thoroughly

This is a very important step in that you can see a lot of valuable information on how the school accepts and rejects people. You can see several things, such as the size of the most recent incoming class, the percentage of in-state students, the percentage of out-of-state students, etc. This is important because you can get a great idea of whether or not your odds are higher of being accepted based on how they accept students. Some schools are more partial towards in-state compared to out-of-state, and vice versa. Also, these numbers are updated from the most recent entering class so they should be very accurate and up to date. Another thing it's worth noting is to speak to your registrar about any potential affiliations between your undergraduate college and the PT college you want to attend. Sometimes schools have affiliations with each other, and they can help guide you in using those affiliations to your advantage.

Moving along, it's important to KNOW YOUR APPLICATION DEADLINE. I cannot stress this enough because so many times students procrastinate and/or feel like things need to be perfect in their application. During my first round of applying to PT school I fell into this pattern of procrastination and wanting everything to be perfect. For example, I saw the deadline as October 1st and assumed that I could submit it as late as that day. I also was not completely satisfied with my Personal Essay (which I will go over later). THESE ARE CLASSIC MISTAKES. Schools may be looking at applications as they are coming in, and it's important to get your application in as soon as possible. This also shows the school that you are proactive and interested in attending there. My second time applying, I made sure that I applied as early as possible regardless of the application deadline. To do this, I literally started the PTCAS application as soon as it opened for the upcoming year. I don't remember how long it took me to submit everything, but I want to say that I applied as early as 3 months prior to the deadline of my target school. If there is one aspect that helped me dramatically the second time I applied, it was SUBMITTING THE APPLICATION EARLY.

Along with the prior information, the school also includes information regarding its admission requirements. They will definitely list a minimum Grade Point Average (GPA) to apply and the average GPA they accepted in the most recent class. This is important because if you are nowhere near the minimum GPA they require, you have just identified your first weakness in your application. I will include ways to help you strengthen this. It is important to note, however, that schools usually include a list of prerequisite courses which are more applicable to the PT field. Since GPA includes all courses and not just your PT prerequisites, your GPA MAY be lower depending on your strengths and weaknesses. In my personal case, my GPA was above the minimum but below average. However, my prerequisite GPA was above average, which was another way I separated myself from the competition. One other thing that is important to note here is that it goes a long way when you have taken more than the minimum required for prerequisites. This shows the programs that you are motivated and have better aptitude in those subject matters. I will elaborate on this section in much more detail.

When you apply on PTCAS, you must manually enter all of your courses that you attended in your undergraduate studies. This is tedious and time-consuming but necessary to the entire application process. DO NOT DO THIS FROM MEMORY! When you are applying, they will double-check everything with your official transcript (this must also be sent in). I had a copy of my transcript sent to me and sent to PTCAS. Therefore, I had a copy I could refer to and the official copy was on its way to them.

The program will also list the Graduate Record Examinations (GRE) scores required for admission. Just like GPA, some may include a minimum GRE score for each section. Therefore, it's important to meet the minimum. Also, they will list the average scores of the recent students they admitted. You want to use this as a guideline when choosing a program. Just like for GPA, you will also have to manually enter your GRE scores. If you decide to retake the GRE after you have already submitted your application (which is common), I will elaborate later on how to approach this.

It is also important to know if the school you are applying to has an interview process. This can be a KEY element of getting into PT school. This adds a totally different element to the interview process. This information is either present on PTCAS or on the school website.

Finally, know if your desired program has a supplemental application. Sometimes schools will require a supplemental application, which can be any of the following: essays, prerequisite classes, fees, etc. BE SURE YOU KNOW IF THESE ARE REQUIRED. You don't want to have submitted nearly everything and be denied because you have an incomplete application.

Step 3: Get all documents sent in early

Building on my earlier point of submitting the application early, PTCAS requires that they get your transcripts, letters of recommendation, etc. This is important to know because sometimes your alma mater's registrar may take several weeks to send in your transcript. Also, if you have a professor or employer who is slow at writing recommendations, this may delay things. Therefore, I also want to stress to GET ALL DOCUMENTS SENT IN EARLY. Some schools have early admission and others do not. In my experience, regardless if they have early admission or not, you need to get your application submitted early. Even if you plan everything to get there just in time, several factors could potentially delay it. According to the website, processing at PTCAS can take as long as 4-5 weeks! Therefore, once you know the school's deadline, send in the materials early. The first time I applied to school, I was lazy and the documents nearly missed the deadline. My second time, I submitted everything as soon as possible. This is also required for PTCAS to confirm all the class information you entered is legitimate.

There is something else I want to talk about here and that is the common misconception that you need to wait until all documents are received by PTCAS in order to submit your application. The PTCAS application is continually being updated and if everything is entered but PTCAS still has not received anything, it is usually suggested to submit your application. For instance, the second time I applied to school, I was still waiting on my most updated GRE scores. I submitted my application; however, after retaking the GRE, I put my target school down to receive the updated scores. I also emailed the admissions coordinator at the school and updated them directly.

Step 4: Complete the PTCAS checklist

If you've followed the steps up until now, you are probably in great shape, but ALWAYS CHECK THE PTCAS CHECKLIST. This is extremely important because every year things may change. PTCAS provides a checklist for their applicants so that you can cross things off as you complete them. It is easily accessible straight from the PTCAS homepage. This application process is a long one and can take several days or weeks, depending on how fast you enter information. Be sure to check things off the list as you complete them to ensure that you have submitted everything. The first time I applied, I neglected the PTCAS checklist, and I was pretty disorganized when it came to my application. I believe this also resulted in me taking additional unnecessary time to submit everything.

Chapter Summary

First-Time Mistakes:

- Did not get documents in early
- Waited until documents were received and then submitted application
- Did not submit application early
- Did not follow PTCAS checklist

Improvements:

- Submitted all documents early
- Submitted entire application 2-3 months before deadline
- Completed PTCAS Checklist

2

Go to Your Target Program's Open House

___

Now that you have checked out programs and determined which ones you would like to apply to, I highly suggest going to an open house event at each of them. Touring the program ahead of time is very beneficial because it allows you to narrow down your choices of where to apply. An open house is typically organized by faculty and/or current students in the program. The first time I applied, I went to one open house, but I did not take full advantage of it. The second time I applied, however, I went to several, got familiar with faculty and staff, and tried to get as much information as possible.

Step 1: Know accreditation status

It seems like every year new PT schools are being started at universities. If you decide to include one as your target school, it's extremely important to KNOW THEIR ACCREDITATION STATUS. Accreditation is a process used in the United States to assure that students are getting high-quality education. This is done by a group known as the Commission on Accreditation in Physical Therapy Education (CAPTE). A school's accreditation status should be listed on the school's website or on PTCAS, but if it is not, you can look up any school at http://www.capteonline.org/home.aspx. I bring up accreditation status because it may take a while for new schools to become accredited. I'm looking a few years in advance when I say this, but if the school is not accredited, then you're not allowed to sit for the board exam. Therefore, it's crucial to know the school's status. If they are not yet accredited, then ask them about the date when they will be.

Step 2: Know the school's facilities, graduation rate, and National Physical Therapy Examination (NPTE) pass rate

At these open house events a school will typically show you their facilities, discuss the program, and talk about their graduation and NPTE pass rate. All of this is very important information. For instance, I was interested in a school and found out that their anatomy lab was in an entirely different location and that their board exam pass rate was lower compared to other schools. Take it from me, physical therapy school can be tough and very difficult. I couldn't imagine having to run around to different locations to try to make it to class on time.

Next, you want to specifically know the graduation rates of the program. We had 6 or 7 people not complete the program due to personal or academic reasons. This is important to know because you don't want to go to a program that has a high chance of failing because then you have wasted time and money. I looked at it this way, if I fail, I am still responsible for all my student loans. This terrified me, so I wanted to know their specific graduation rate. If the pass rate is at least 80% and above, then it's a good target school.

You also want to know the NPTE pass rate of that target school. This is known as the dreaded "Board Exam." After you graduate, you must take this exam to become a licensed Physical Therapist. Usually, this number is considered strong for a program if it is 90% and above. You want a program that prepares you to pass this exam; otherwise, this can be a massive source of stress. Personally, my school modeled the curriculum around passing this exam so that when it came time for its students to take it, they felt very prepared.

Finally, one thing that I believe helped me during PT school was my school's low student-to-faculty ratio. This ratio is important because it will show you the number of students per faculty member. I like this because it also allows the faculty to accommodate more unique learning styles when the number of students is lower. I am more of a visual learner, and my professors could tailor things for me and others who were also visual learners. If there are too many students per faculty member, this can become more difficult.

Step 3: Ask questions!

Everything should be laid out fairly clearly on PTCAS and during the open house. However, sometimes schools will have additional things that are not listed or discussed. Therefore, I suggest asking as many questions as possible. At the open house you can find out everything, such as cost, credit hours per semester, etc. This is all valuable information that can help you determine if this school is the right one for you. One thing I want to put some emphasis on is the distance you would be commuting to school. I saw a correlation between distance traveled to class and difficulty while in the program among my peers. I am not saying you should completely disregard a school if you have to commute an hour to go there. But I do want to make sure you are aware that between studying, assignments, and clinicals, your free time is valuable. Some other important things to ask about include housing, local attractions, and upcoming events in the school. Show an interest in the school and the surrounding areas. This will also help you get a big picture of what life in the area is like.

Chapter Summary

First-Time Mistakes:

- Only went to one open house
- Was not familiar with target school, faculty, and staff

Improvements:

- Went to several open house events
- Became familiar with target school, faculty, and staff

3

Know the Interview Process

Some schools require an interview so that they can finalize their selection process for the incoming class. This can be a very nerve-wracking experience, but a good interview can really set you apart from other applicants. Believe it or not, being invited to the interview is a massive compliment because the school already believes that you are qualified. In this section I want to go over some interview tips that I did not use the first time and things I implemented the second go-around. At my first go-around I was only invited to one interview, and I really had no idea what to expect. I was thrown off by questions because I hadn't prepared properly. The second time I applied, I was invited to two interviews, but this time I had assembled a game plan and felt very prepared.

Step 1: Group interview

One school I had an interview with required a group interview with prospective students and then an individual interview with a member of the faculty. The purpose of the group interview is to see how you interact with prospective students and your abilities to work together.

Unfortunately, I only experienced doing a group interview during my second application, but I felt like I learned a great deal about the process. During my group interview, a case study was given and the group had to decide how to work on it together. Whether this is the format of your group interview or not, there are some strategies that I implemented during mine. You will most likely have to introduce yourself, so I suggest preparing an introduction ahead of time. I just practiced saying my name, my alma mater, and one interesting fact about myself. If you want, you can practice saying a few things about yourself so that you have options.

Second, if they are asking the group questions, I suggest answering first a few times. Even if you are shy and timid, just go for it. If you seem reluctant to speak and hardly talk, this usually does not help you. Whether the interviewer here is faculty or a current student, they are taking notes on how people respond during the questions. Therefore, speaking first every once in a while helps to separate you from the pack.

Third, agree and try to work with the group as well as possible, even if you disagree with what is being said. I tried my best to do this by making friends and making some small talk prior to the process. This is important because, like I said, earlier they are looking to see how well you work with others. This is a very important thing during your time in PT school because you constantly work in groups.

Finally, when it comes time for questions, make sure you ask brilliant ones. What I mean by this is pay absolute attention during the entire process and ask things pertaining to the subject at hand. This is important because if you ask a question that has already been answered, that will look bad! They want to see that you are an active listener and that you can formulate some excellent questions along the way. Asking a question that has already been answered never looks good.

Step 2: Individual interview

If your school offers individual interviews with faculty and staff, this is EXTREMELY important. You need to know your potential interviewers' interests, research, and fields of study. During this interview, they will give you a chance to ask questions and it's impressive if you can bring up the interviewer's current research, fields of study, etc. During my first go-around I reached the interview round and knew absolutely nothing about any of the faculty members. When it came time for questions, I am sure I asked some general questions that did not separate me from anybody else. My second time applying, I was checking my school's website and learning everything I could about my potential interviewers. It sounds very extreme, but this really benefits you. I asked specifically about that professor's newly published research project. I knew this would look good on my behalf and it was something I was genuinely interested in. In another interview I had, I knew my interviewer was involved in volunteer work with people who had amputations. These are things that professors are passionate about and love to talk about. It also separates you from other prospective students because it will make you memorable.

Step 3: Why do you want to come here?

You will ABSOLUTELY get some version of this question during the interview. There are many PT schools these days, and you need to have a great answer to this question. "I like it here," is not a good enough answer! You need to know the school backwards and forwards. What separates this school from others you have looked at? Why would this school be a great fit for you?

When I was asked this question, I named all of the positives I saw in the school compared to others I had looked at. First off, I was interested in the school because of their low student-to-faculty ratio. Some schools have a limited number of faculty members, which can be tough when you need answers to questions or help with assignments. Therefore, it was important to me to have access to many faculty members in relation to class size. Also, all of the faculty at my target school were current practitioners in the field of Physical Therapy. Sometimes faculty will only take on an administrative role, so I really liked that they were current in their treatments in a clinical setting. This ensures that they are up to date on treatments and related healthcare information.

Another thing I responded with was how much I liked that the anatomy lab, classrooms, and labs were all under one roof. As I stated earlier, some schools have these facilities in different locations and all the running around can add stress to an already stressful environment. I also liked the condition of the facilities. Some schools have older facilities and are out of date. The admission board enjoys hearing how nice their facilities are compared to the competing schools.

I want to add that during my interview the second time around I had experience working with an alumnus of that school in the clinical setting. This can be very important, especially if you have direct access to alumni from your target school. This can not only help you because it gives you a connection, but it can also show you how alumni from that school function in the working world. This was another example of why I wanted to attend my target school. I felt like my experiences showed me how professional their alumni are.

Finally, does the target school you are being interviewed for do any extracurricular things? My target school had a weekend activity where you could volunteer to help children with disabilities with pool therapy. I had zero experience with aquatic therapy, but this sounded like something fun and beneficial for me. Also, my target school participated in service projects in other countries, which I wanted to be a part of. Find out what types of extra activities the school is involved with and bring them up during this part. If they do not participate in anything of this sort, find differences that separate them from other places. By doing all of this, the target school realizes that you have really done your research and that you genuinely want to attend for multiple reasons.

Step 4: Why do you want to become a Physical Therapist?

This is another guaranteed question during the interview, and you need to have a great answer. They'll ask you, "Why do you want to become a Physical Therapist instead of any other healthcare profession?" Therefore, it's important to know exactly how a Physical Therapist operates day in and day out and how this compares to other professions. First off, I responded with how much I like the frequency of seeing people. This differs from other healthcare fields because as an outpatient Physical Therapist, you will most likely see people several times a week. Being a Physical Therapist allows you to help a person in many different ways, including musculoskeletally and even psychologically. Finally, I loved the idea of becoming a Physical Therapist because I had seen examples of how people who had gone to Physical Therapy were able to get their lives back. I had seen amazing things over the years, and I wanted to be a part of that. This is important because it allows you to build rapport with the patient.

Another reason I was drawn to Physical Therapy was that you are functioning a lot in a team-based setting. This was important to me because it allows you to speak with physicians, surgeons, other PTs, etc. and gives you a great approach to patient treatment. During PT school and during your PT career, you will have to communicate with all different fields on a regular basis. When done correctly, the team-based approach can be incredible and very beneficial.

Finally, as a Physical Therapist you can treat any type of patient population. For instance, every Physical Therapist has education on how to treat all types of patients, from pediatric to geriatric. You also get extensive education on working with people with neurodegenerative diseases, cardiopulmonary issues, you name it. If some day you want a change, you can have it.

All of these reasons why I went into the field of Physical Therapy can be used, but I encourage you to look into other reasons, find out why you want to become a Physical Therapist, and make your explanation unique.

Step 5: Other things you should know

It is not uncommon to get questions regarding current events in the Physical Therapy world. I personally did not get any of these questions, but I know some colleagues who did. One subject that comes up repeatedly in PT school is the topic of Direct Access. Direct Access is essentially the patient's ability to access a Physical Therapist without a physician referral. Historically, a patient was required to go to a physician first and then to a Physical Therapist. Direct Access is a big benefit to the field of Physical Therapy because it allows a PT to be more autonomous. I suggest looking up Direct Access and learning more about it ahead of time.

Other things I encourage you to look up are: Medicare Cap for Physical Therapy, Physician-Owned Physical Therapy Practices (POPTS), and any current updates that the American Physical Therapy Association (APTA) has to offer. These issues are always changing, so I do not want to elaborate on the current decisions because they may change down the line. However, I will say that it's important to know these subjects because even if you are not asked about them, you can always ask your interviewer about them. They will give you a chance to ask them questions at the end and if you want, you can always bring these up. I brought up the Medicare cap because that was something I had learned about in my time working. Showing interest in the field and the current events will always allow you to separate yourself from others.

Chapter Summary

First-Time Mistakes:

- Did not know entire interview process
- Did not properly prepare for the question, "Why do you want to come here?"
- Did not prepare great answer for "Why do you want to be a Physical Therapist?"

Improvements:

- Researched entire interview process more than once
- Had great answers to usual questions
- Knew current topics pertaining to Physical Therapy

4

Looking for GPA Weaknesses and Improving Them

We all know that GPA is a big determining factor when it comes to applying to PT school. As I stated earlier, it's important to first know the GPA requirements for your desired school. Even if you have a stellar GPA, it is important to look for holes in your GPA. The admission board will be looking for weaknesses and you should try to eliminate as many as possible.

Step 1: Look for Cs or Lower

First off, look for any classes for which you received Cs or lower. This is important because it is exactly what the admission board will do when going through their hundreds of applications. This is very important if you have Cs or lower in prerequisite classes. These prerequisite classes are there for a reason; they will provide you with some base knowledge when you start the curriculum in PT school. The admission board will also base your chances of success in PT school on how you performed in these courses. That is why there is a lot of emphasis on them. If you have not graduated yet, look up your college's policy on retaking classes if you have any grades that you need to strengthen. If you have graduated and are no longer able to take the class at the school, do not be discouraged. I retook a class at a local community college and that was sufficient to strengthen my application. If you are retaking the class, be sure you earn an A!

Personally, I had one C in a prerequisite class the first time I applied and I am convinced that this was a big red flag. I did not improve on this grade and this C lingered on my application. When it came time for the interview process, this was brought up and I was asked about it. I knew right then and there that this was a major weakness in my application. My second time applying to school, however, I retook a class at a local community college. Before you go this route, I would ask the school you are applying to if this is allowed. Typically, it is (as it was for me), but it never hurts to ask. There are many benefits to using a community college as opposed to a big university. The most obvious is that you will save a lot of money when you go this route. Also, community colleges tend to be more flexible and have class times that are doable if you are working full time.

The number of prerequisite courses will also play a role in the strength of your application. In the prerequisite section for some institutions, they will give you options of which classes will fulfill a requirement. Sometimes there will be 5 or 6 to choose from. In my case, I had my undergraduate degree in Biology. Therefore, I had taken several of the listed classes, when in actuality the program only required one of them. An admission board will see this and recognize that you have a great understanding of the subject if you have taken more than just the bare minimum requirement. I was told that the admission board usually accepts the highest grade you received for that category. For example, let's continue with the Biology category. If you got a C or lower in General Biology but received an A in Cell Biology, the admission board will tend to factor in the A in the prerequisite GPA. The lower grade will still linger, and I do suggest improving on that.

Chapter Summary

First-Time Mistakes:

- Having a C or lower in a prerequisite class
- Not retaking it prior to applying
- Bare minimum of prerequisite classes

Improvements:

- Retake prerequisite classes earned C or lower
- Take multiple prerequisite courses in each category

5

Looking at GRE Scores and Improving Weaknesses

If the Graduate Record Examinations (GRE) is required for you to apply to your target PT school program, I want to outline some things that helped me in this area. The test has changed since I took it years ago, but you obviously want to get the highest score possible. Personally, I never did very well with the Verbal section of this test but always had an easier time with the Quantitative section. Therefore, I knew that I needed to emphasize a lot on the Verbal section in order to make sure I was competitive. You should apply these same rules. Are you more of a Verbal or Quantitative Person? The first time I took the GRE, I tried to just use flashcards to learn words and things that I was not very good with. This resulted in me knowing words but not being able to apply them towards the test format. The second time I took the test, I used preparation books and took as many practice GREs as possible.

Step 1: Buy GRE prep books

The first thing I recommend is purchasing multiple GRE prep books. I went with books from Kaplan and Princeton Review. They have practice tests, practice problems, etc. These books are the most beneficial because together they offer hundreds to thousands of practice problems. The best way for me to begin using them was to take a practice GRE. This allowed me to identify my weaknesses right away, which was unsurprisingly the Verbal section. Therefore, that section was my main focus throughout the time I was studying. I also want to point out that several Physical Therapists told me that schools focused more on the Verbal section. Now, I cannot be certain if that was true or not, but I was able to improve on my Verbal score when I took the test a second time and I know that it really did benefit me.

Step 2: Focus on your weak areas

The first time I applied to Physical Therapy school, my score was enough to surpass the minimum requirement, but it did not turn any heads because it wasn't spectacular. My average GRE score combined with several holes in my application did not make me appear as an ideal candidate. Like I mentioned earlier, my Verbal score was subpar. Therefore, I implemented a few strategies that allowed me to raise it a few hundred points.

First off, when I was doing practice problems, if there was any word of which I had to guess the meaning, I looked it up. I then made a note card and reviewed these cards each week to make sure the words were solidified in my head. Next, I tried to read as many books as possible.

This sounds easy enough, but I realized that I was lazy reader. Finally, I put nearly all of my focus on practice problems from the Verbal section. These three combined strategies really helped me.

If you are weaker for the Quantitative section, I suggest doing as many practice problems as possible. Learn the specific concepts that are recurring in these problems and memorize their processes. If there are any specific processes that you find hard to memorize, you can implement the note card strategy I used for the Verbal section. Nevertheless, my best advice is to do as many practice problems as you can. If you get something wrong, then learn why. When I retook the GREs a second time, I hardly focused on the Quantitative section and yet my score improved compared to the first time. I believe this happened because I did so many practice tests.

Some final notes for the GREs: I noticed that they like to recycle some questions. If you do a lot of practice tests and practice problems, there is a chance that you may see some familiar questions on the actual GRE. If this happens, make sure you read the entire question carefully. Sometimes they may repeat a question and change a single thing that will alter the answer completely. Just make sure you read everything carefully and make the best decision you can. Also, if you feel like a preparation course may benefit you I know several people who have used those to help boost scores as well.

Chapter Summary

First-Time Mistakes:

- Not taking multiple practice GRE tests
- Not using multiple GRE preparation books

Improvements:

- Bought and completed many GRE preparation books
- Took as many practice GREs as possible
- Focused mainly on weak areas that needed improvement

6

Letters of Recommendation

Each program requires that you have letters of recommendation for your application. Schools usually specify who these letters should come from: your professors, physical therapists you have volunteered with, etc. Most schools require at least one professor and one Physical Therapist. These recommendation letters can be the difference between a strong application and a weak application because the word of academic professionals carries a lot of weight.

Step 1: Get more than the minimum required letters of recommendation

First off, even if schools just require one letter of recommendation from a professor and one from a Physical Therapist, it is important to get more letters. The more people you have in your corner supporting you, the better off you are. The first time I applied to PT school, I provided the bare minimum of letters of recommendation, and I can tell you that this hurt me. When I applied the second time, however, I had recommendation letters from four people in total. This was a significant improvement, not only because the number was higher, but also because I had a recommendation letter from a person who'd graduated from my target school. I will elaborate on this more, but this can be very influential compared to a Physical Therapist who graduated from another program.

Step 2: Pick Physical Therapists and professors who know you the best

This is one of the most crucial steps of getting your letters of recommendation. The better the person knows you, the more they can write and schools will absolutely be able to tell the difference. One thing that actually plays a major role is a professor that you have research experience with. This is something I was unable to do for both my first and second times applying to school because I had zero experience doing an outside research project with a professor. If you have this already, absolutely have them write you a recommendation letter. Your target PT school will really appreciate the fact that you have experience doing academic research. Even though I did not have research experience, I picked two professors who saw me work very hard in their classes and ones that I had great relationships with. I also made sure these professors taught some of the prerequisite classes for PT school.

Make sure you choose Physical Therapists that have seen you the most in the clinical setting and know how you interact with people. Make sure that they know how badly you want to get accepted. The first time I applied, I volunteered at a few places but did not really develop a personal relationship with the Physical Therapists there.

The second time I applied, I had been working with many Physical Therapists, always asking them questions, and always showing my interest in the field. This gives them a lot of information when it comes time for them to write you a letter of recommendation.

Step 3: Ask them at least 3 months in advance

Sometimes it can take a while to write these letters of recommendation, which can delay the process. Therefore, following the same themes as before, it's important to ask them to write you a letter of recommendation with plenty of time to spare. I would personally meet with them in their office rather than sending an email because it is more personal. Another thing that is helpful is to also send them your resume so that they can build a better picture of what your extracurricular activities are. My first time applying I asked for my letters of recommendation very late in the process. I also did not send my resume to be reviewed by them, and I believe their letters were not as strong as they could have been because of this.

Chapter Summary

First-Time Mistakes:

- Minimum letters of recommendation
- No therapists were alumni of target school
- Asked about writing my letter of recommendation later
- Did not send resume
- No research experience with professor

Improvements:

- More than bare minimum letters of recommendation
- Alumni of target school wrote letter
- Sent resume
- Asked 3 months in advance to write letter

7

Diversifying Physical Therapy Observation Hours

To apply to PT school you will need to have a minimum number of observation hours. These hours are important because they will give you some great experiences in the field of Physical Therapy before you even start going to school.

Step 1: Diversify your PT Experience

You need a minimum number of observation hours in order to apply to PT school, which you might already know. These requirements are put in place so that students see what happens on a daily basis and they know 100 percent that they want to become a Physical Therapist. Personally, I always had an interest in the rehabilitation of outpatient orthopedic injuries. Therefore, at my first go-around, I volunteered at an outpatient orthopedic clinic near my house in order to meet these hours. I met the bare minimum of hours necessary to submit my application. My school had an interview process and when I went in for it, I was asked if I had any experience in the inpatient world. This caught me off guard, because I had none whatsoever, but this is a massive portion of Physical Therapy. Physical Therapists work in nursing homes, hospitals, inpatient rehabilitation centers, etc. I had my mind so set on working in the outpatient orthopedic world that I overlooked these other settings. Schools are concerned with a diverse experience of different settings because in PT school you learn, are tested, and have clinicals in ALL settings. Therefore, it's important to volunteer at as many different types of settings as possible. I believe that my lack of experience in the other PT settings was another major hole in my application that affected me negatively.

Since I lacked the diversity of volunteer hours, I volunteered at a local nursing home. Here I learned a great deal about another side of physical therapy. Believe it or not, I really enjoyed it too. It was different but beneficial. I learned things during my time there that I supplemented my education with while in graduate school.

Step 2: Exceed the minimum number of observation hours

Another major hole in my application was that I volunteered the bare minimum of hours. I was naive about the process and thought that would suffice. I am willing to bet that the admission office interpreted doing the bare minimum as me being a slacker. Like I have mentioned before, always try to go way above the minimum required hours. If I could have done this entire process over, I would have volunteered frequently at different settings during my undergraduate studies. This would have also helped me build my network of Physical Therapists and could have saved me from getting rejected the first time.

My second time applying to PT school, I had really focused on working on these weaknesses. First off, I was able to work at an outpatient orthopedic clinic full time. These positions are often called Rehabilitation Technicians, or "Techs," for short. They are beneficial positions to get experience in a real-life setting. If you are able to get paid during your time, it is the best of both worlds. I want to point out that some schools MAY NOT accept paid hours. This is very important to know ahead of time, and you can find this information on PTCAS. My target school accepted paid hours so I was good to go there. I knew this would give me a lot of hours that I could use as clinical experience because I was working directly with a PT every day. Now I could meet and exceed the required hours by a long shot.

Step 3: Try to work with a Physical Therapist who graduated from your target program

If you can find a PT who has graduated from your target program, this is the ideal situation for your observation hours. You have probably heard the saying, "It's not what you know, it's who you know." That is partially true when applying to PT school because the people on the admission board may have a good working relationship with this graduating PT. This person will also be able to tell you how the program is and answer any potential questions you have (which is usually a lot). This PT is also a great person to write a recommendation letter and/or email to their prior professors on the admission board. When I graduated, I remember that a professor told us as a group to let them know if we had anything great to say about a potential applicant. Typically, schools do this because they know their graduates should have a good understanding of how a person will do in their program.

The first time I applied to PT school, I knew absolutely no graduates from their program. I remember that I went to the interview process and was speaking with other applicants. Several told me that they either volunteered or worked with graduates from the program. I commonly heard, "Oh yeah, I worked with them a lot and they just graduated from here, they wrote me a letter of recommendation." I knew right then and there that this was another hole in my application because several people had connections and I had zero.

The second time I applied, I made sure this hole was fixed. During my full-time position as a Rehabilitation Tech, I knew that a PT who worked there had graduated from my target school. I remembered all the people who had told me about working with graduates of their program, and I knew I needed to work hard for this person and get to know them a lot better. Initially, I was not working with this person, but I asked my boss if I could get some hours with them to strengthen my application. My boss fortunately told me I could, and I split time between them and the regular PT I was working with.

Chapter Summary

First-Time Mistakes:

- Experience in only one setting
- Doing the bare minimum of hours
- No experience with graduates of target program

Improvements:

- Volunteer in as many settings as possible
- Exceed the minimum hours required to apply
- Work with program graduate

8

Writing a Unique Personal Essay

The Personal Essay is a section on PTCAS that requires you to write an essay based on the topic they list. When I applied to school, they wanted to know about my experiences in the world of Physical Therapy and why I wanted to become a PT. The personal essay is a way for you to separate yourself and be unique from other applicants. Therefore, it's important to go in with this mindset and to try and compose an essay that fits this mold.

The first time I applied to PT school, I wrote about how Physical Therapy had helped me with a prior injury. I thought that would be helpful because I had experienced it personally. When I talked to people about their applications, I found out that a lot of people wrote about their times as athletes and how they had overcome injuries with Physical Therapy. Hearing this I realized that what I had written was not necessarily the best way to differentiate myself from the crowd. Now, I'm not discouraging you from speaking about your injuries and experiences rehabbing them if you have done so. What I am suggesting is that if you want to talk about your personal experiences being a patient, try to include some other experiences that make you unique.

The second time I applied, I went in with this mindset. I wrote about how on a volunteer service trip I realized I wanted to help people for the rest of my life. I talked about how great it felt for me to help people and that I wanted that feeling day in and day out. I also spoke about how, during my time as a rehabilitation technician, I met so many great people and they told me how great a Physical Therapist I would be. I listed specific examples but used fake names so that the person could remain anonymous. Finally, I talked about the team-based setting in Physical Therapy. I love the team-based setting and the benefits of a collaborative approach to treatment.

Chapter Summary

First-Time Mistakes:

- Did not write about unique story
- Used generalized reasons why I wanted to become a Physical Therapist

Improvements:

- Used unique experience in clinical setting
- Spoke about several instances of why I wanted to become a Physical Therapist

9

"The Squeaky Wheel Gets the Grease"

In my experience this was the most stressful portion of the entire process: the time after interviews and after everything is submitted. During this period you are waiting for a decision from your school on whether or not you were accepted. I remember constantly checking my emails and being extremely stressed out during this time. The first time I applied, I remember waiting weeks and weeks without hearing anything and being just terrified about the unknown. Believe it or not, there are some specific things you can do during this time to help improve it.

First off, when I talk to current students in this predicament, I always ask them, "So have you emailed them?" They usually tell me no and say something along the lines of, "Well, I don't want to be annoying." I went in with that mindset the first time I applied, and I was not accepted. The second time I applied, I spoke to my boss about it and asked his advice. He simply told me, "The squeaky wheel gets the grease." What he was trying to tell me was that if you are persistent enough, you will get attention. What I suggest is that after everything is submitted and after the interview process (if your school has one), you wait 2 weeks. Usually, they will tell you when the deadline for decisions is, but if you have not heard anything after 2 weeks, I would send an email to the contact person who is the admissions coordinator. If you are not sure what to write, this is the exact email I sent when I was applying. I've left out the names so that everyone remains anonymous.

Hello Dr. So and So,

I was wondering how the waitlist process is going. What date should I hear by before I need to contact the University? Has the new class already been decided or are students still being moved up from the waitlist? If you could let me know, that would be great.

Thank you!

Sincerely,
Nick Gallo

It's important to always address the professor by Dr. and then their name, but here is a good example of how you can ask about their current process. It's also common to take a class or retake the GREs after you have had the interview, so my second time around, I emailed the admissions coordinator directly updating them on my scores so that they did not have to wait on PTCAS. For example, here is another way I contacted my school regarding this:

Hello Dr. So and So,

I would just like to update you on my status regarding retaking Class A. I have registered for the Spring semester. I will let you know as soon as I have any additional information. Thank you, I hope you had a great holiday!

Thanks!

Sincerely,
Nick Gallo

The same can also be done for GRE scores. What I am getting at is that as soon as there is a person you can contact directly, it's important to fill them in with emails so that they are continually updated. This not only informs them faster, but you become a name they are familiar with.

Chapter Summary

First-Time Mistakes:

- Did not contact target school enough after everything submitted and interview process
- Was not known among faculty and staff

Improvements:

- Emailed frequently regarding application status
- Continually updated admission coordinator regarding GRE scores/classes retaking

10

What to Do If Not Accepted

———

The second time I applied, I was not 100 percent convinced that I would be accepted even with all the improvements I had made. This is a true story. The night before I was accepted, I was looking up alternative graduate school programs. I will never forget the day I was accepted. It took until February 28th (it was a leap year). I know other people who heard even later than February. If you are still on a waitlist or have not heard back from a school, it's really easy to panic and start to second-guess yourself. Through communication with the admission board and performing these strategies I have outlined, your application will improve. If you are not accepted, it's a terrible feeling and I have been there. Following the advice from before about being more assertive, I emailed the person at my target school and asked them how I could improve my application and increase my chances of admission. Here is a copy of the email I sent:

Hello Dr. So and So,

My name is Nick Gallo and I was on the alternate list for last year's physical therapy program interviews. I am working as a Rehabilitation Technician at X clinic under Y therapist to gain more experience in physical therapy and will continue to do so throughout the course of the year. I will also be retaking my GREs to try and boost my scores. "Target School" is my number one choice for physical therapy schools, and I was curious if you could tell me what I could do to strengthen my application even further. Also, would you happen to know the dates of the open houses for this upcoming year? If you could let me know, that would be fantastic!

Thank you,
Nicholas Gallo

The admission chair reviewed my application and told me exactly how I could improve it. If you are not admitted the first time you apply, do not lose hope. This is an excellent way for them to tell you exactly what to work on. It also makes your name familiar for them. By implementing this strategy along with the others I have written about, you can strengthen your application, separate yourself from the competition, and become more confident in the Physical Therapy application process.

Now It's Your Turn

After reading this publication, you should have everything you need to improve your Physical Therapy school application. I wanted to keep this short and sweet with all relevant information because I know how valuable your time is when applying to schools. I hope that you have found this informative and helpful in your journey to being accepted into Physical Therapy school. Applying to Physical Therapy schools can be a very stressful process, but I can assure you that it is absolutely worth it once you are accepted. It is now your turn to go and put these strategies to your advantage. I want to thank you for reading my guide and wish you much luck in the application process!

References

PTCAS
http://www.ptcas.org/home.aspx

CAPTE
http://www.capteonline.org/home.aspx

About the Author

Nicholas Gallo is a board certified Doctor of Physical Therapy. He has helped countless patients in his career and continues to practice Physical Therapy on a full time basis. He is also a cofounder of Physical Therapy 101.

Additional Resources

For more information, visit my website at www.physicaltherapy101.net. Here we have resources on various pathologies. This website is continuously updated to provide up to date treatment and is a great resource for practitioners, patients, and prospective Physical Therapists.

Subscribe to my YouTube channel https://www.youtube.com/c/PhysicalTherapy101. Here we produce free treatment videos for patients and healthcare providers. This is also a great visual aid for treatments described above.

I have another publication that you may also find interesting:

Posture Pain: Key Strategies to Stay Pain Free at Your Desk and in Life – I discuss the optimal computer station setup to maintaining ideal posture, exercises to perform to reduce pain, and ways to implement these strategies in other scenarios.

P.S. If you have enjoyed this book and found it resourceful, please leave a helpful review on Amazon.

Made in the USA
San Bernardino, CA
23 December 2019